ABCreeps

A Spooky Alphabet Book

Written by Brendan McWhirk
Illustrated by Marissa Rogers

Ghosts use spirit boards,
and monsters growl.
Zombies groan,
and werewolves howl.
Mortals speak freely as they please,
once they learn the ABCs.

A IS FOR "APOCALYPSE"

The horsemen arrive,
sunken and grinning.
Is the APOCALYPSE an end?
Or a brand-new beginning?

B IS FOR "BLOOD"

Shrink down the craft,
enter through laceration,
protect the BLOOD cells,
destroy the mutation.

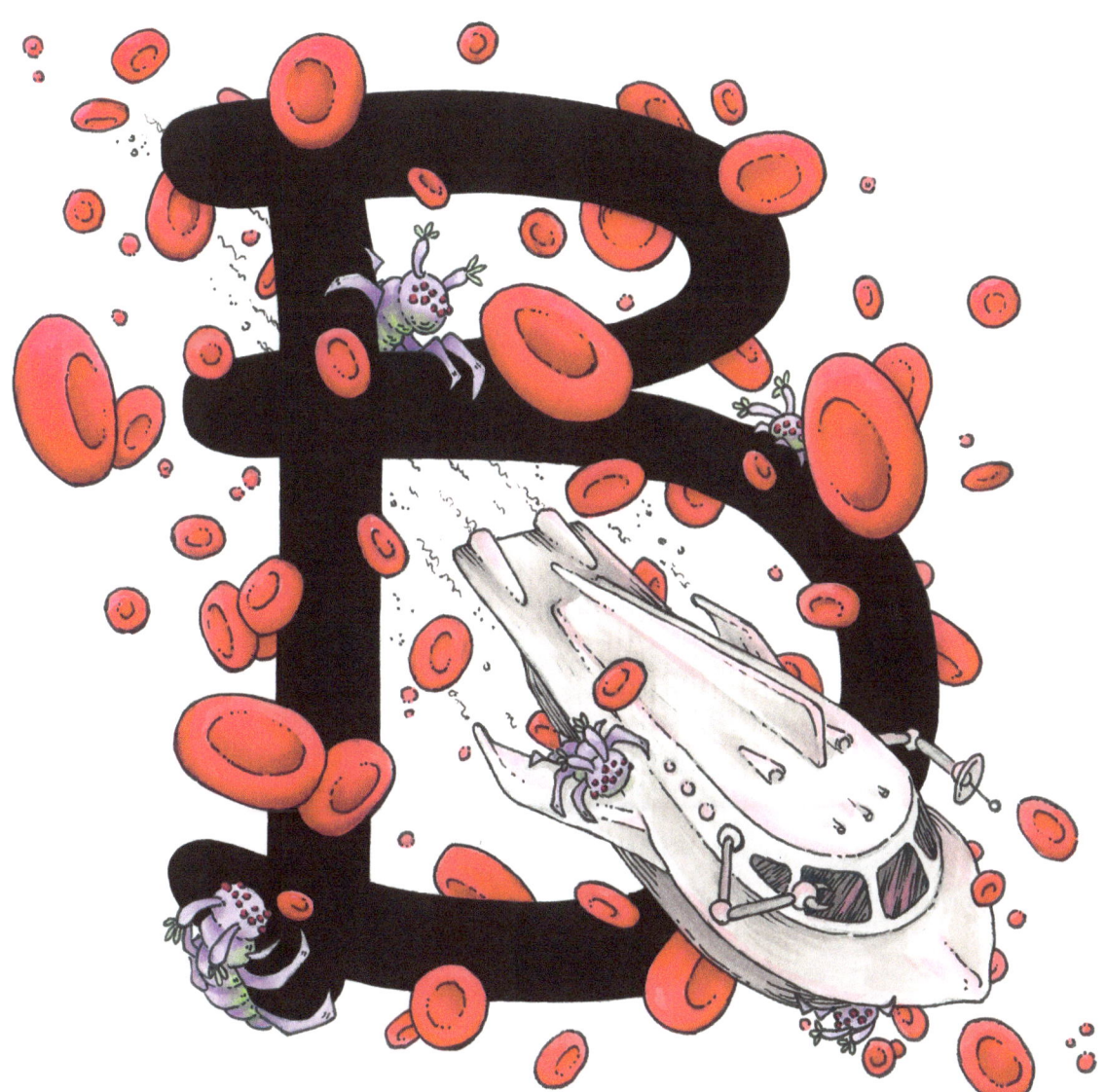

C IS FOR "CANNIBAL"

A moist human sandwich,
go on and try it,
always served fresh,
on the CANNIBAL diet.

D IS FOR "DEMON"

From tiny sharp claws,
to the tip of each horn,
the DEMON never chose evil.
That's just how he was born.

E IS FOR "EXTRATERRESTRIAL"

Escaped from containment.
Call a code red!
EXTRATERRESTRIAL outbreak!
Now it wants you dead.

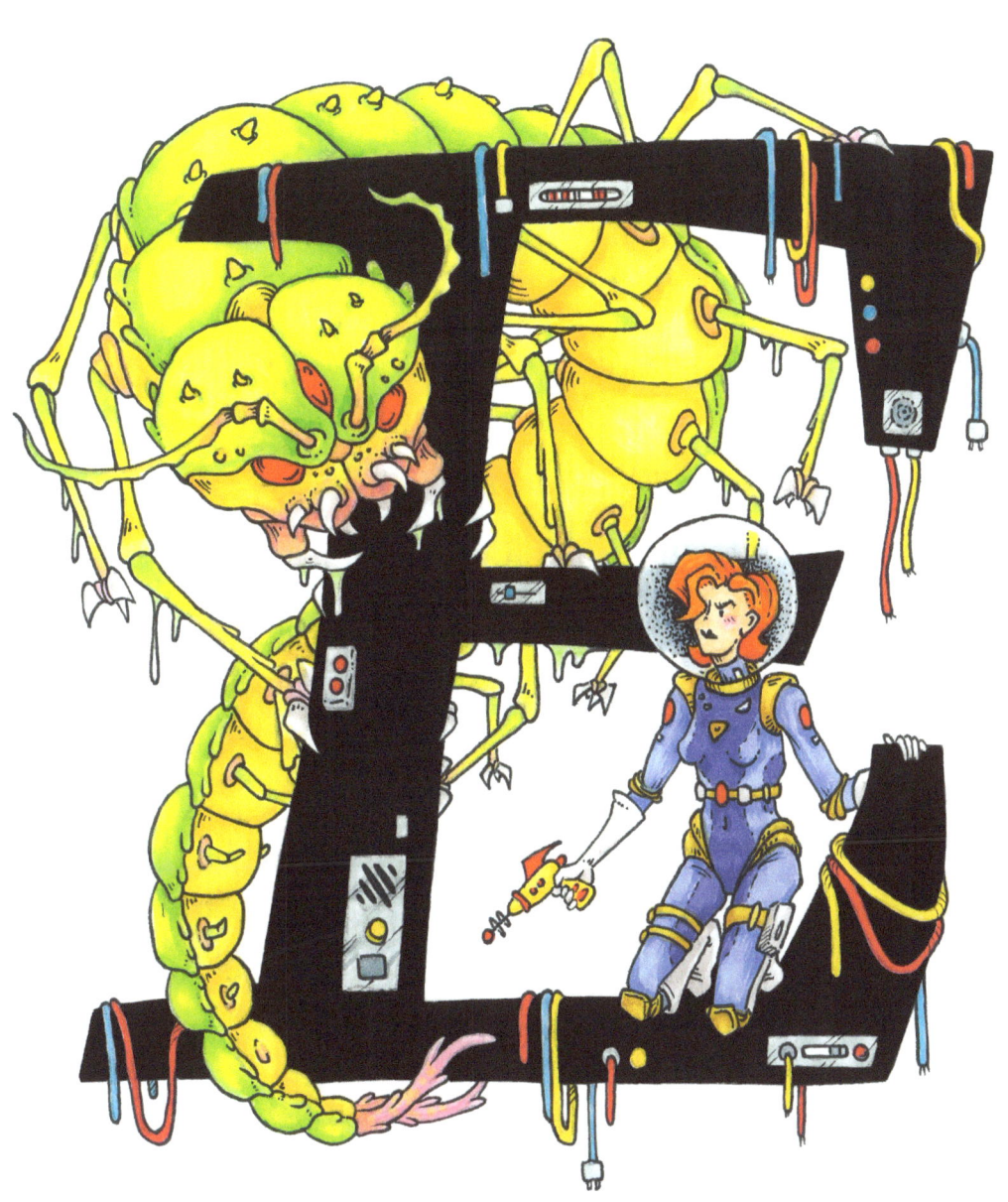

F IS FOR "FUNGI"

In the forest lay still,
a corpse to be found,
covered in FUNGI,
reclaimed by the ground.

G IS FOR "GARGOYLE"

A GARGOYLE of stone,
till the last beam of light.
A mere statue by day,
has a heartbeat by night.

H IS FOR "HAUNTED"

Elegant and Victorian,
the realtor found what you wanted.
She however failed to mention,
your new home is quite HAUNTED.

I is for "INSECT"

Pinned down on a board,
dried out for display,
this INSECT once fluttered,
but those days went away.

J IS FOR "JACK-O'-LANTERN"

Guiding trick-or-treaters,
in costumed attire,
the JACK-O'-LANTERN glows,
with Halloween fire.

K IS FOR "KRAKEN"

Far more than a pirate's tale,
submerged in ocean blue,
the tentacles of a monstrous KRAKEN
rip vessels in two.

L is for "LOBOTOMY"

Strapped down in a madman's chair,
the patient contract signed,
the procedure was for free,
but the LOBOTOMY cost your mind.

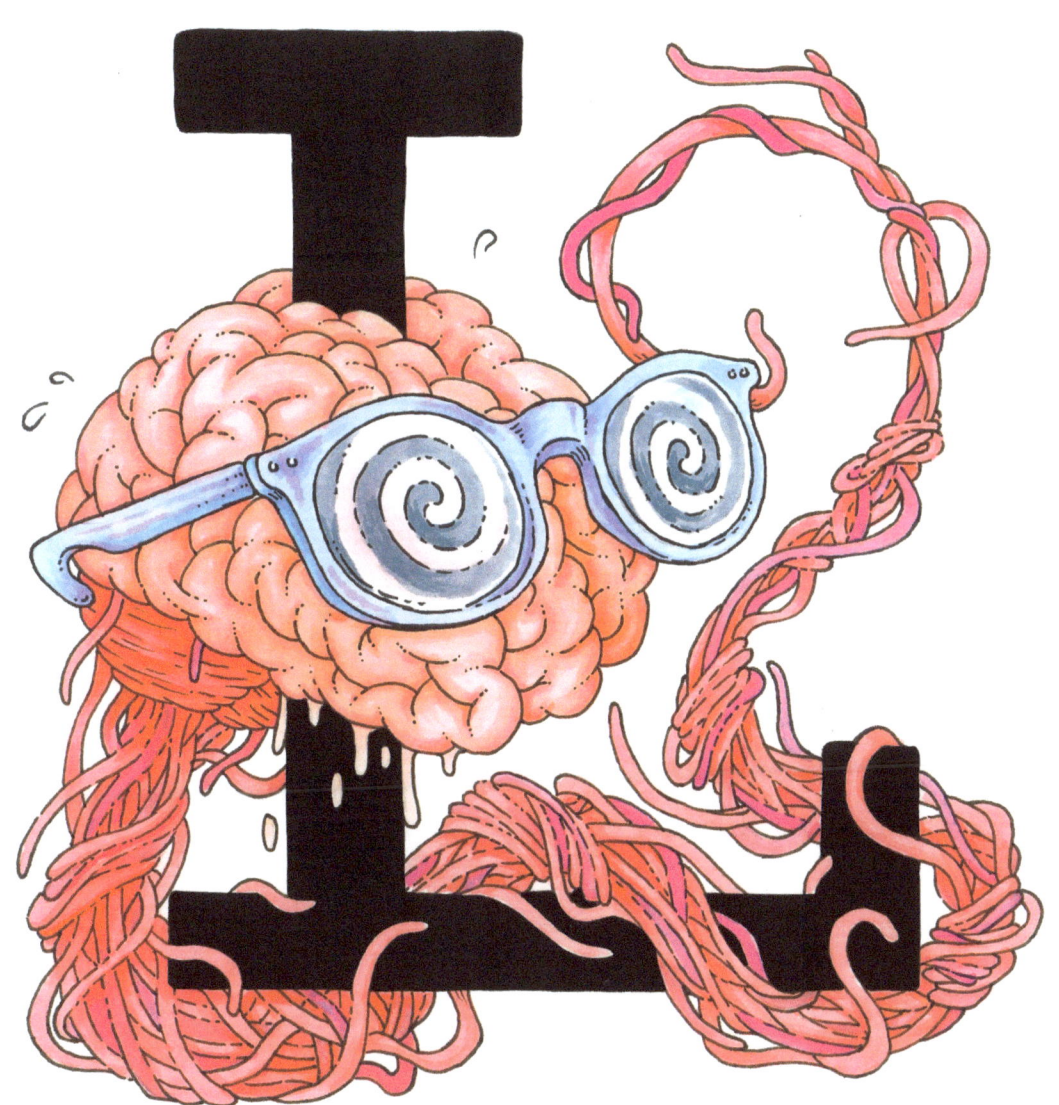

M IS FOR "MUMMY"

The brochure said "Explore Egypt!"
not "Meet your certain doom."
But you woke an ancient MUMMY,
and you're trapped within his tomb.

N is for "NYMPHS"

Alluring guardians,
of water and wood.
Cross the NYMPHS,
and go missing for good.

O IS FOR "OBITUARY"

An OBITUARY is a notice of death,
a bio of one's demise.
Left behind are those they loved.
Please try to sympathize.

P is for "PHOBIA"

Your mind is but a big top,
where a PHOBIA can thrive.
The more attention you feed it,
the more the clown's alive.

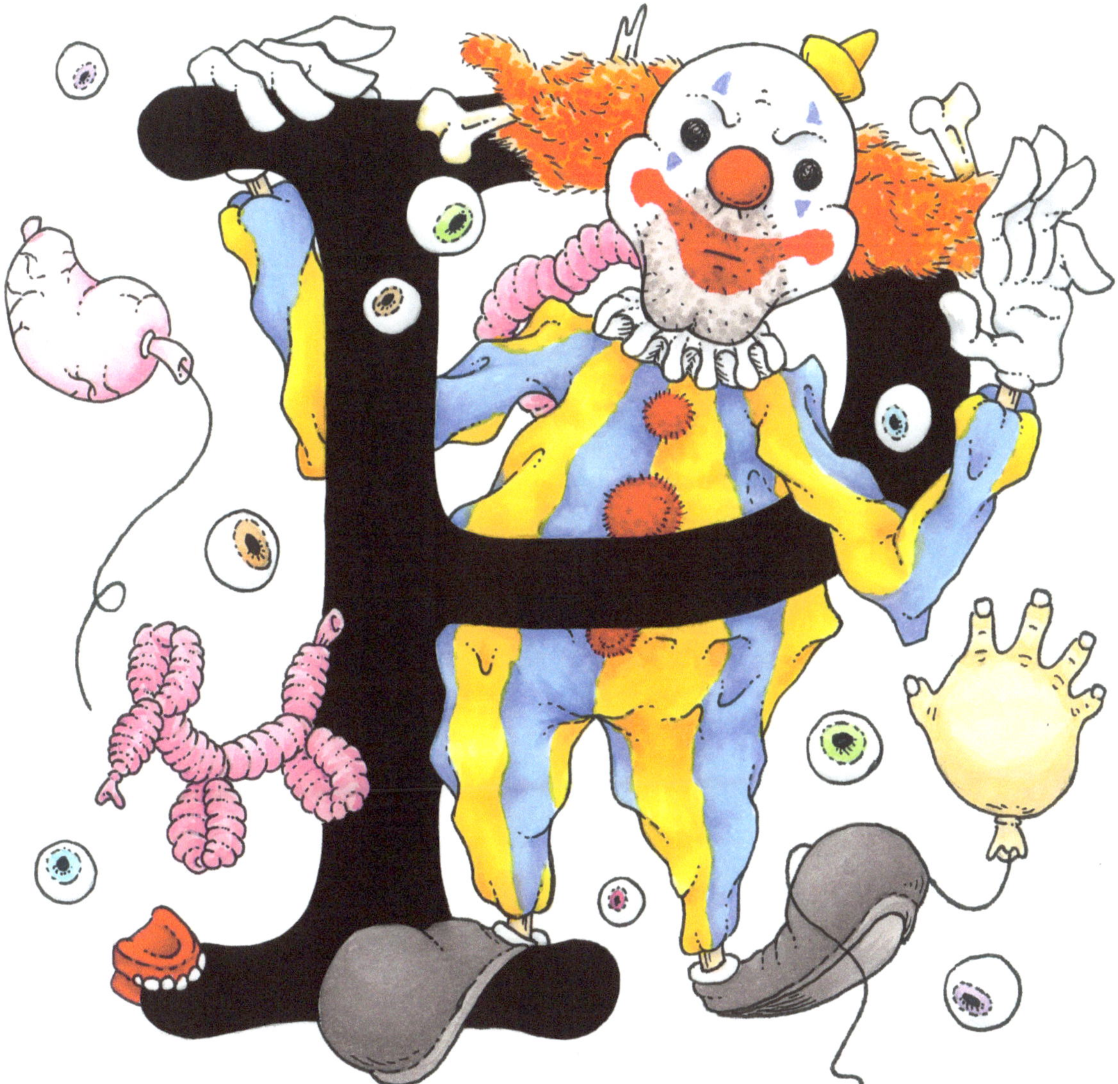

Q IS FOR "QUINTUPLETS"

Pretty porcelain QUINTUPLETS,
each possessed by ghosts.
But kids are much preferred to dolls,
so please send them new hosts.

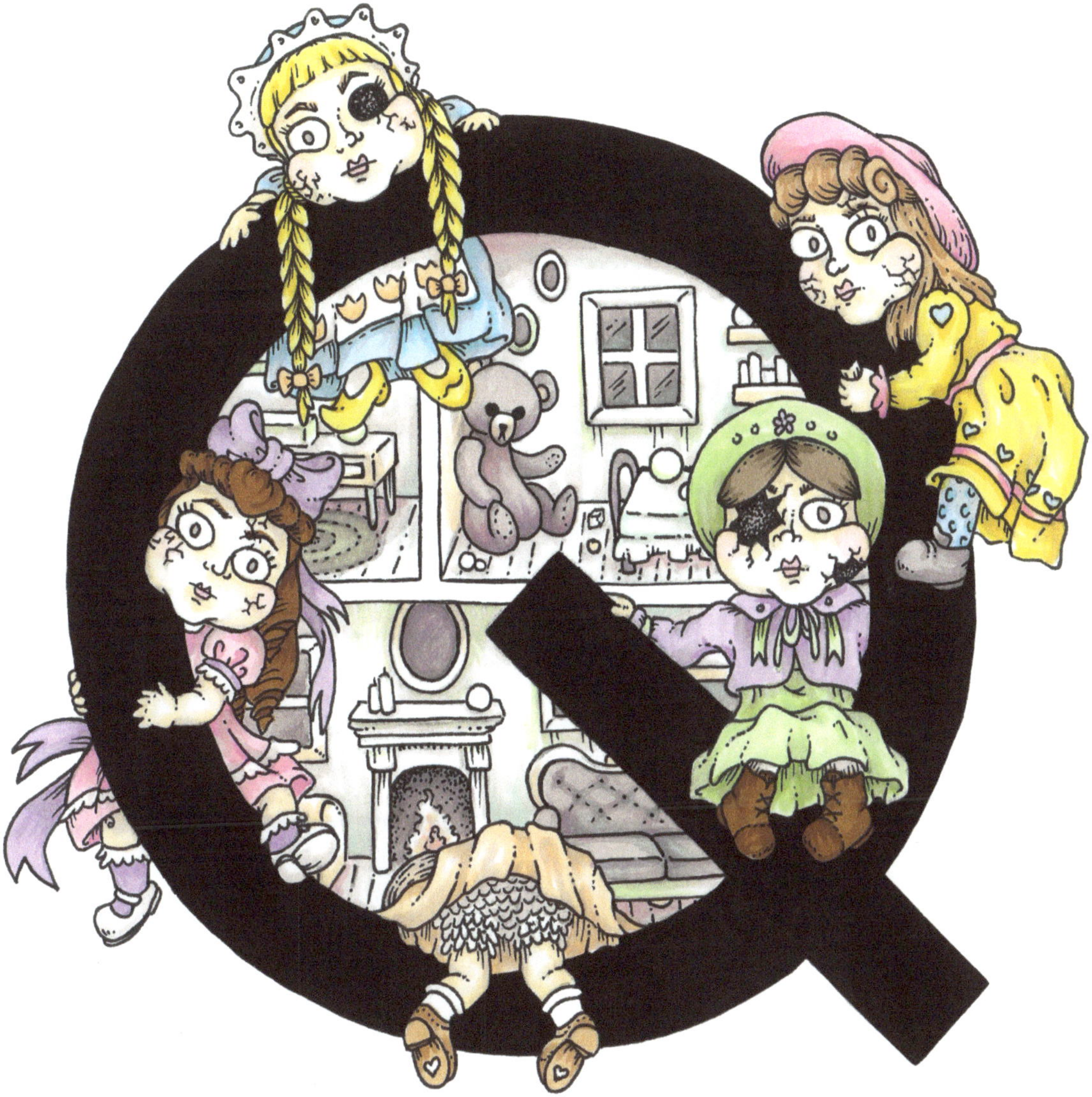

R IS FOR "RODENT"

They overrun the sewer system,
below the city street.
A rabid RODENT and his many friends,
are right beneath your feet.

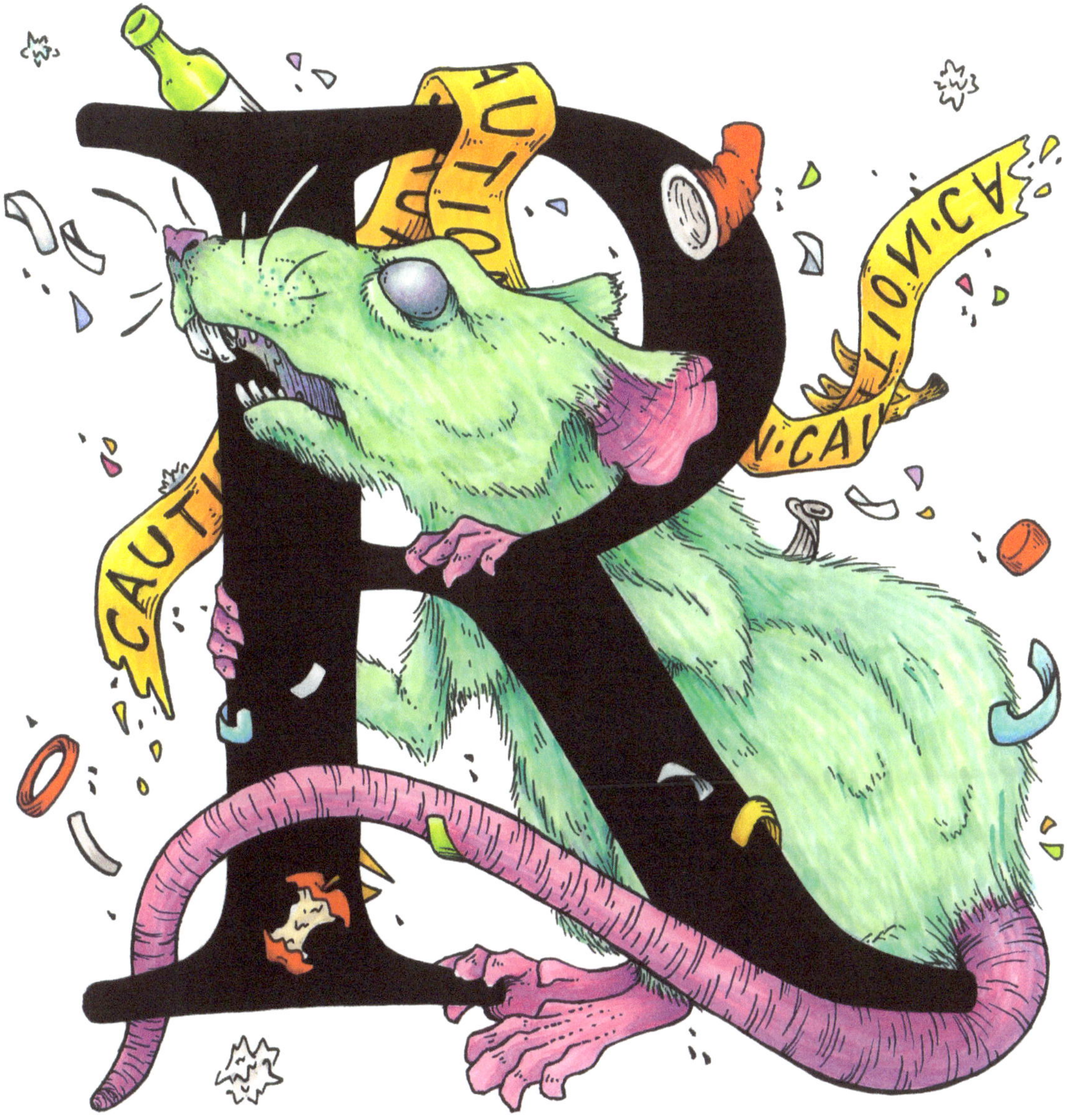
CAUTI
N·CAU

S IS FOR "STAB"

One knife can make a crime scene,
but obsession can make a few.
One STAB can start a gruesome hobby,
bid your old life adieu.

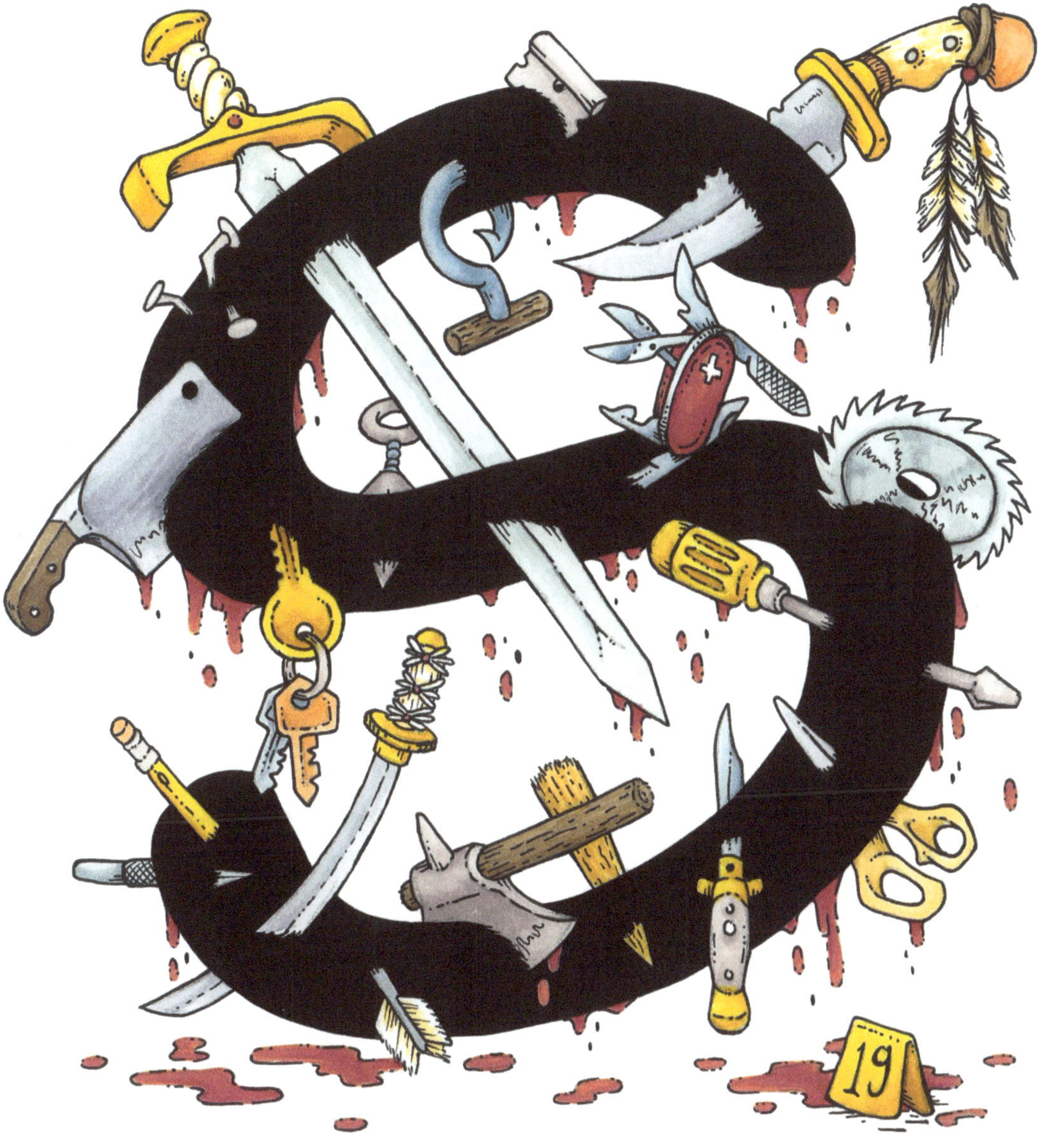
19

T is for "TEETH"

Some TEETH are sharp and some are wise,
a jaw-ful of selection.
And once they fall they're quickly claimed,
a fairy's foul collection.

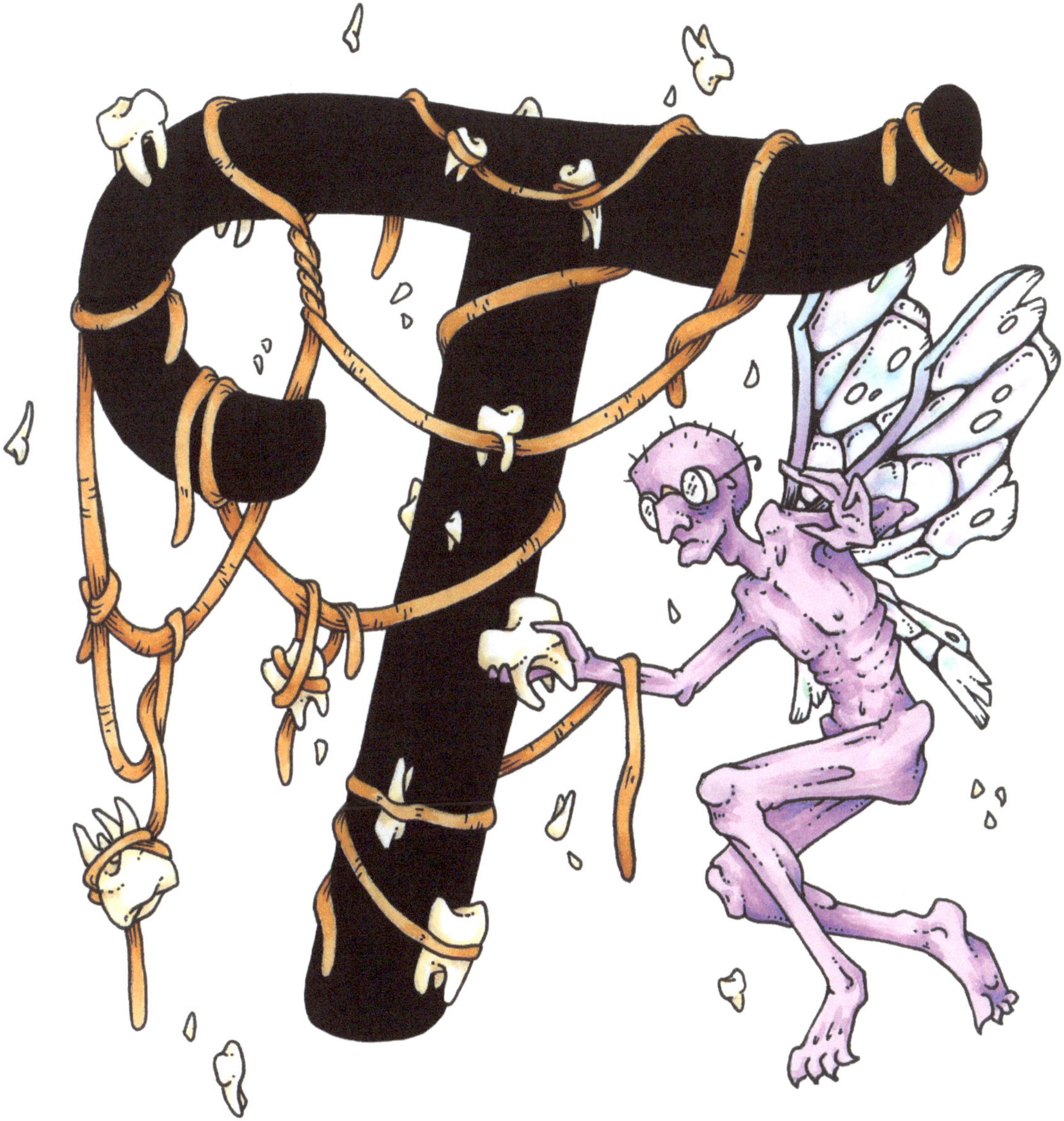

U is for "URN"

Don't mourn the ones you lose,
for life's a celebration.
Their body's dust inside the URN,
destruction from creation.

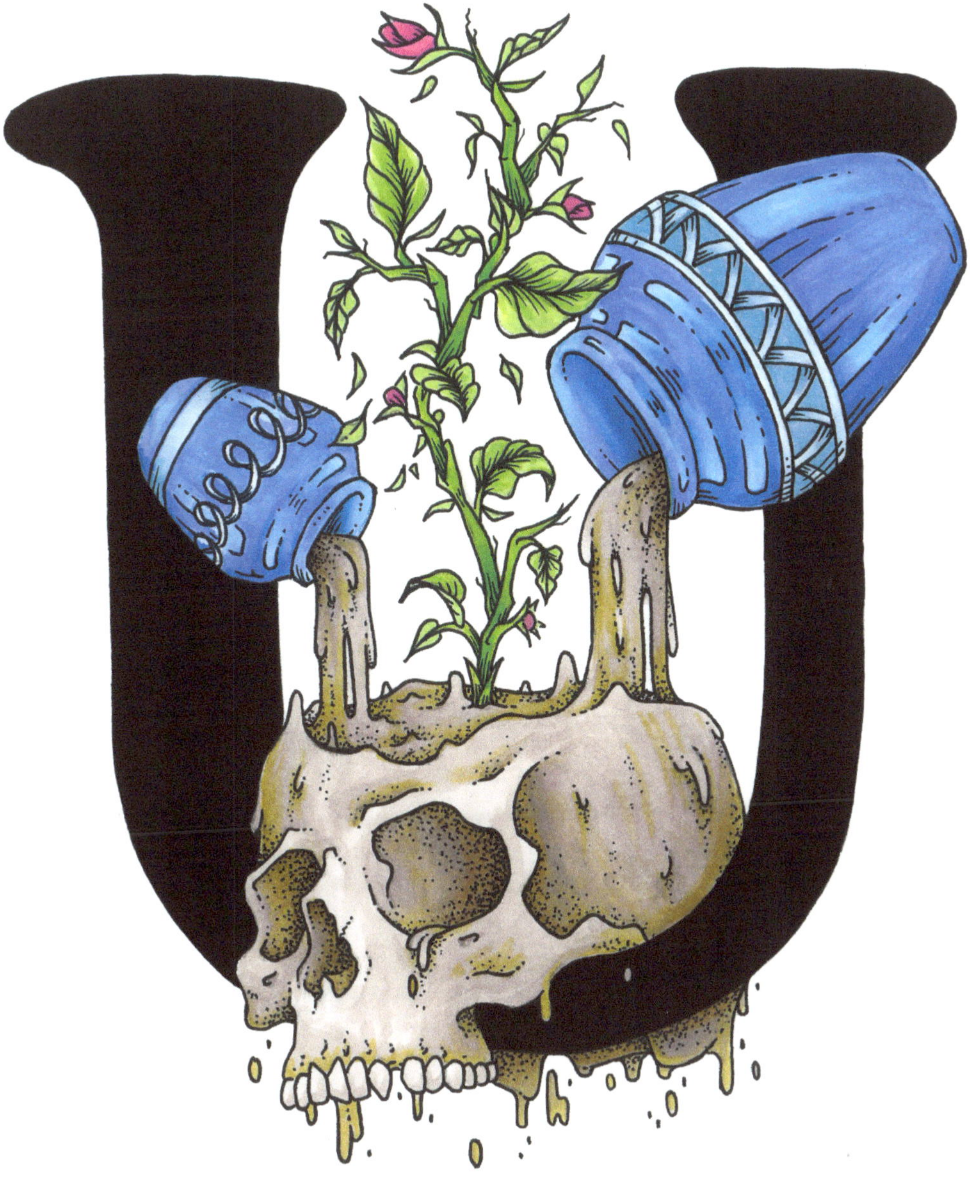

V is for "VENTRILOQUIST"

A VENTRILOQUIST act leaves
audiences wanting more.
But at night he knocks 'em dead
and has critics on the floor.

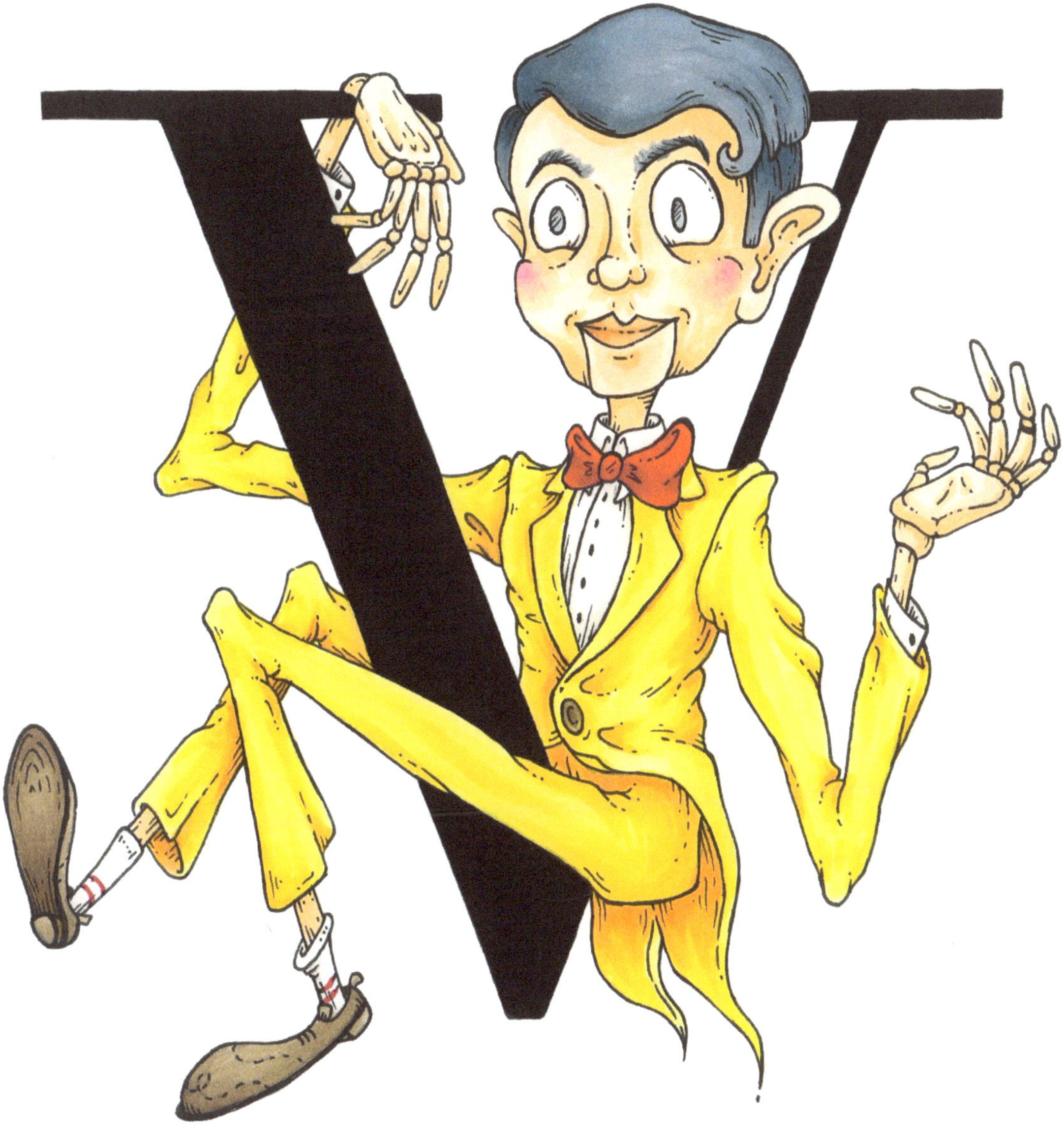

W IS FOR "WARTS"

WARTS can spread quickly,
a spongey, calloused sight.
From a witch's nose to the backs of toads,
they go bump in the night.

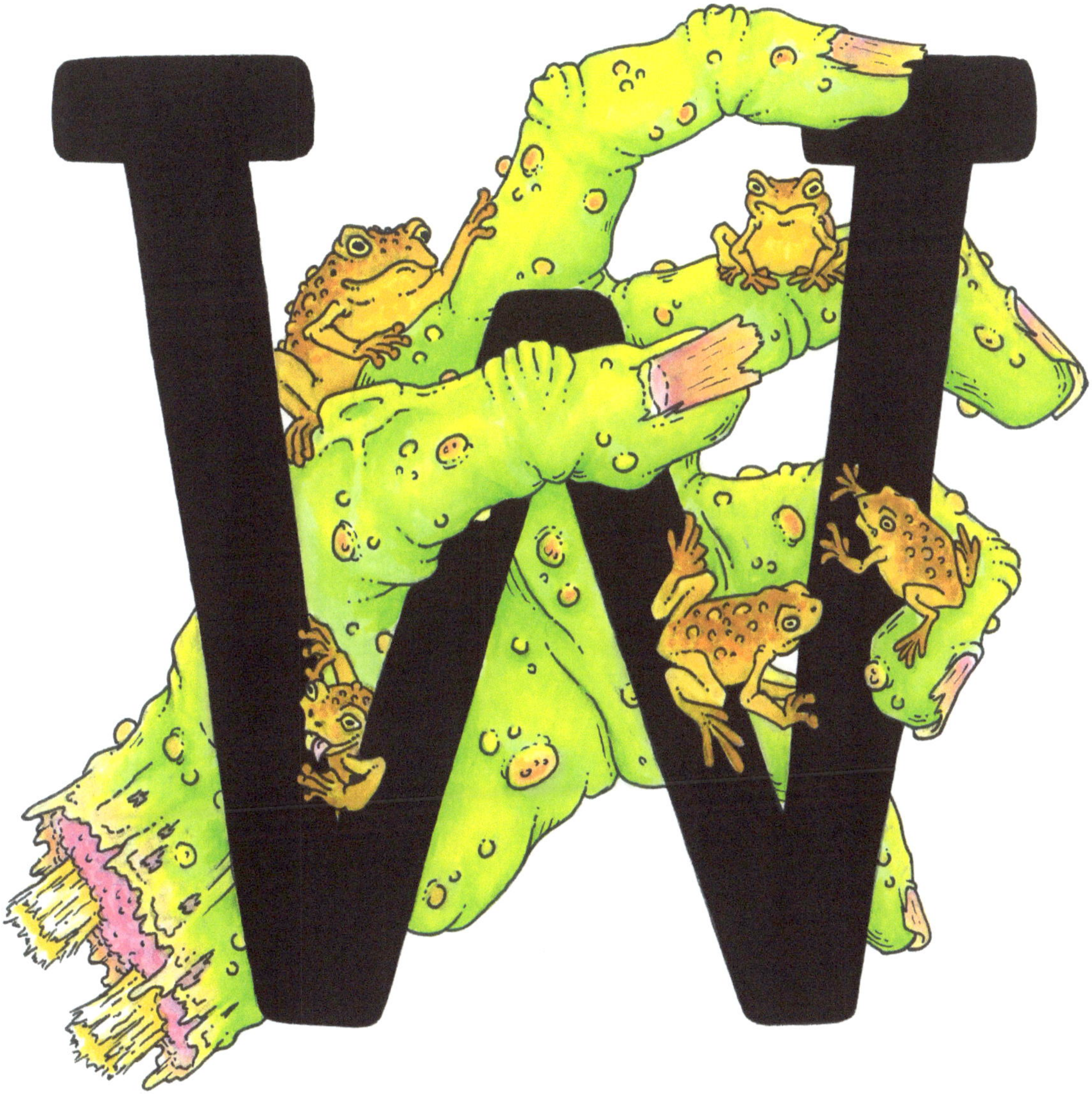

X IS FOR "X-RAY"

An X-RAY reveals
what the naked eye can hide:
Organs, guts, and goo and bones
that fill us up inside.

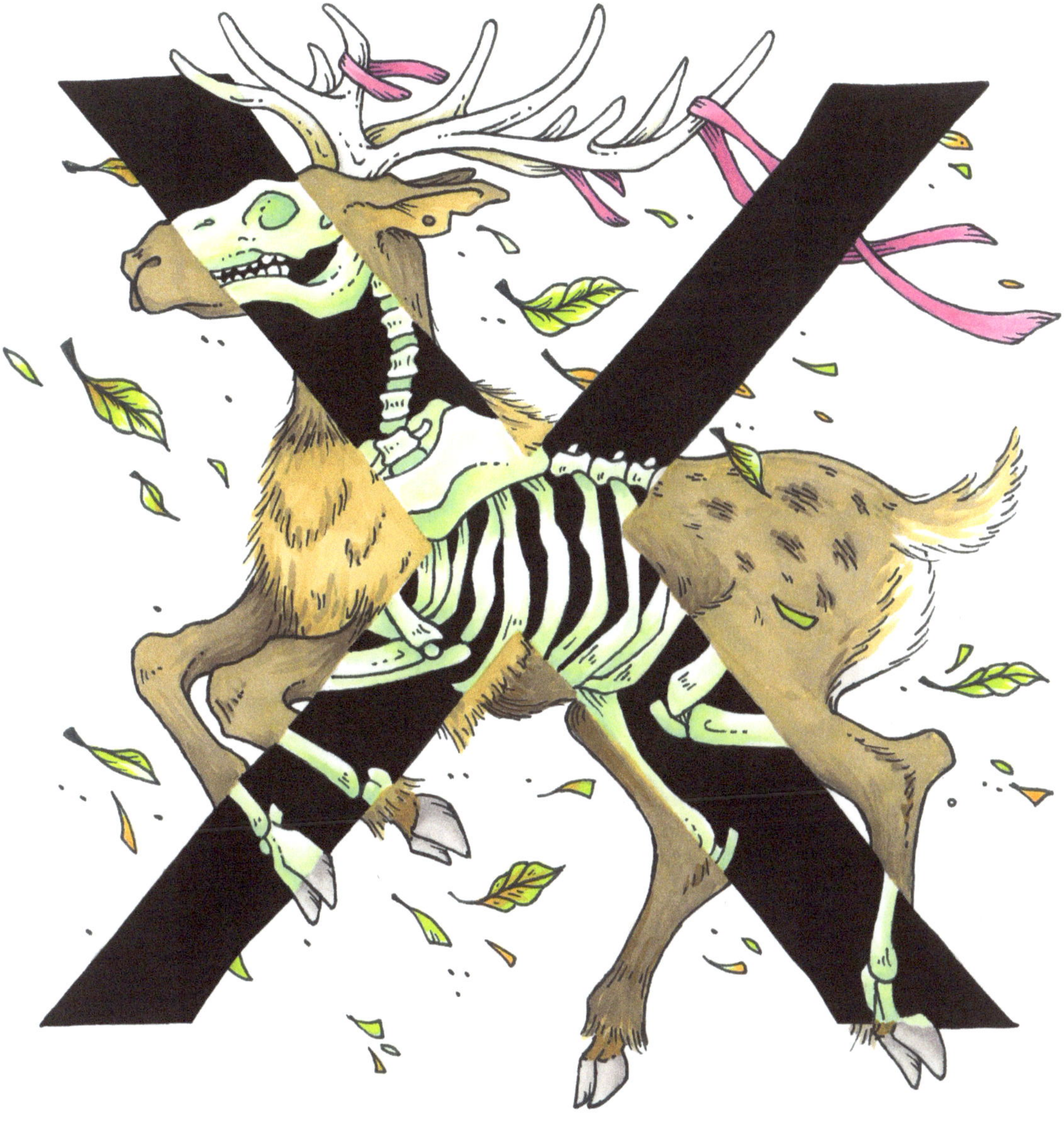

Y is for "YETI"

Bellowing roars echo
from a snowy mountain range.
For up there lives a fearsome YETI,
mythical and strange.

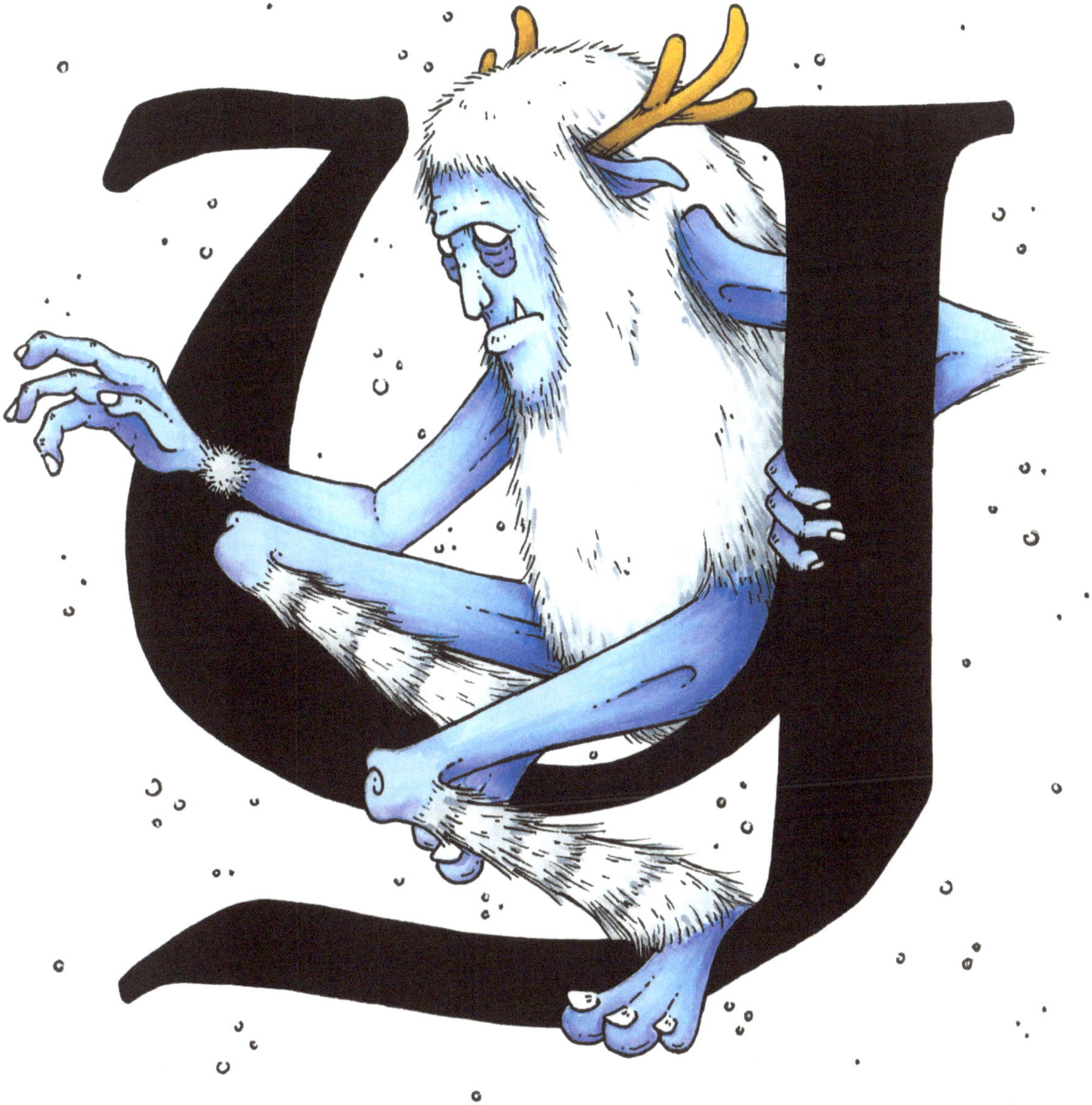

Z IS FOR "ZYGOTE"

A single-celled organism,
bound to split in two.
The monster ZYGOTE will grow up
and eat humans just like you.

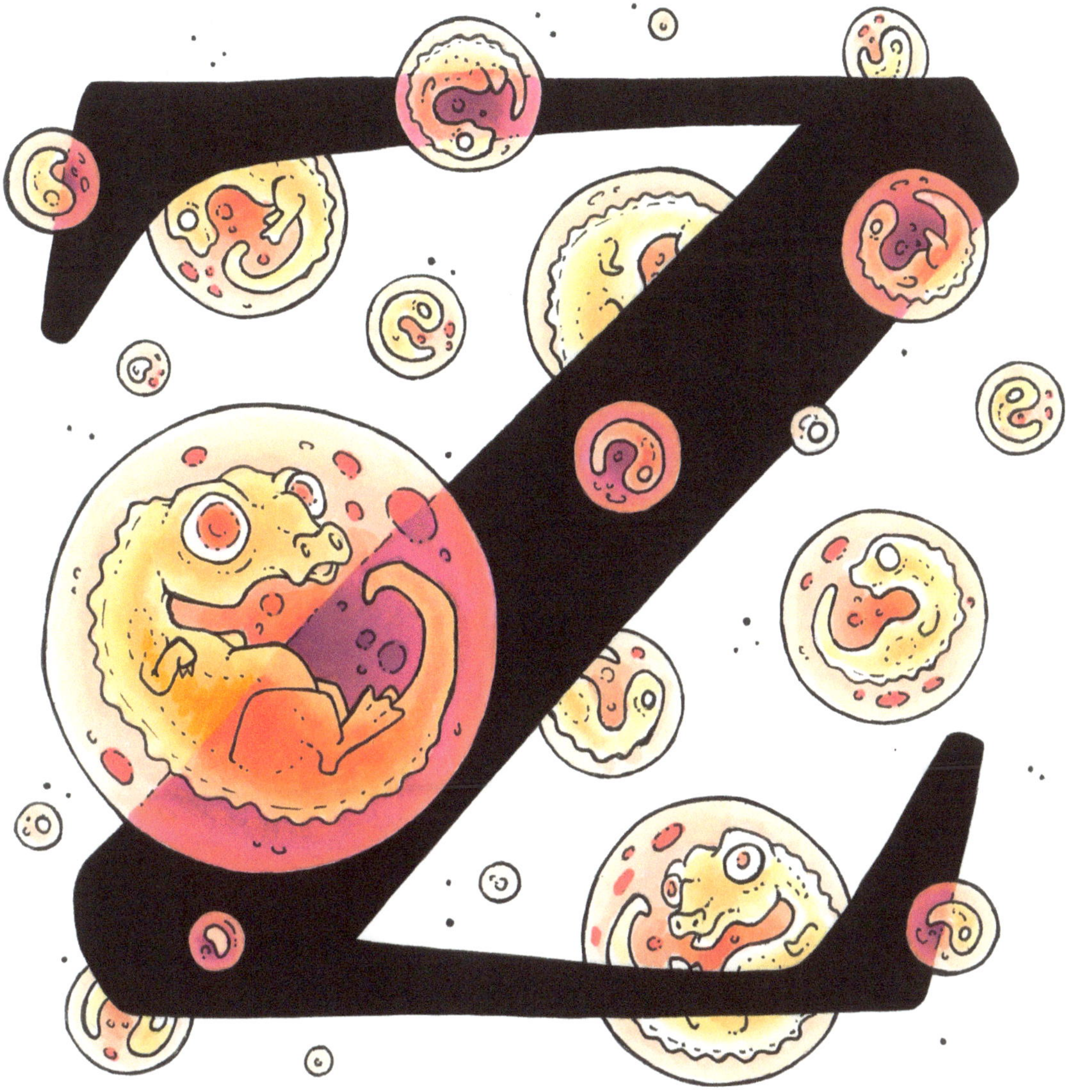

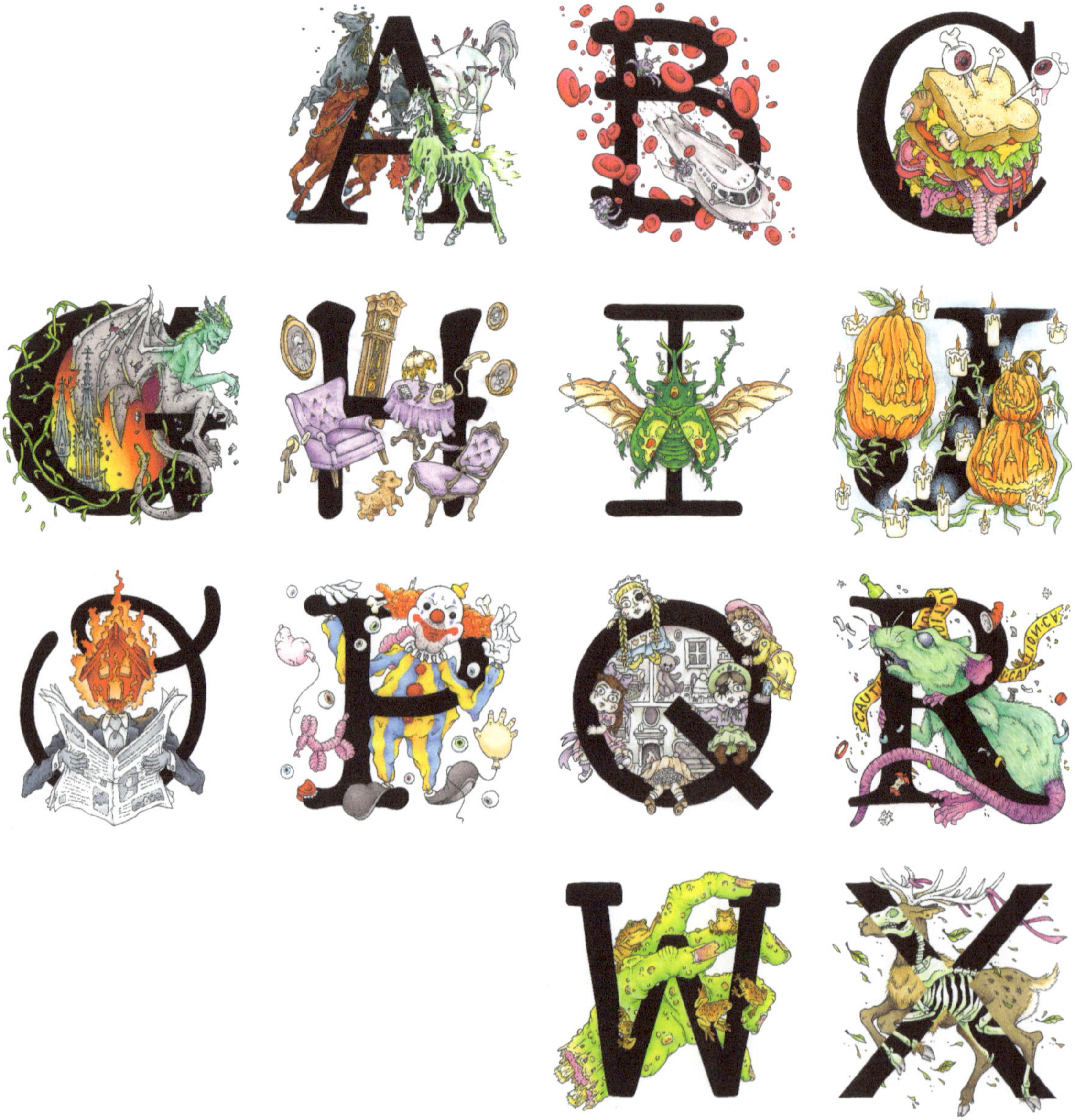

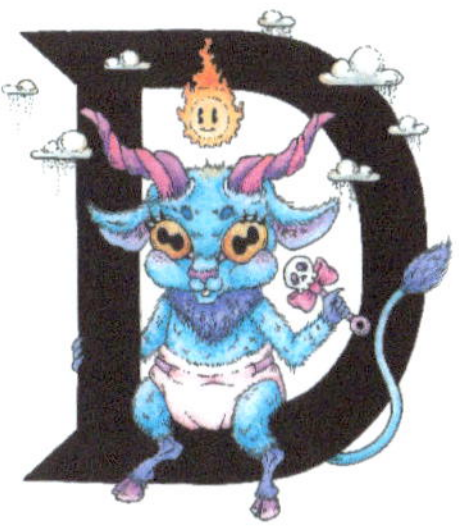
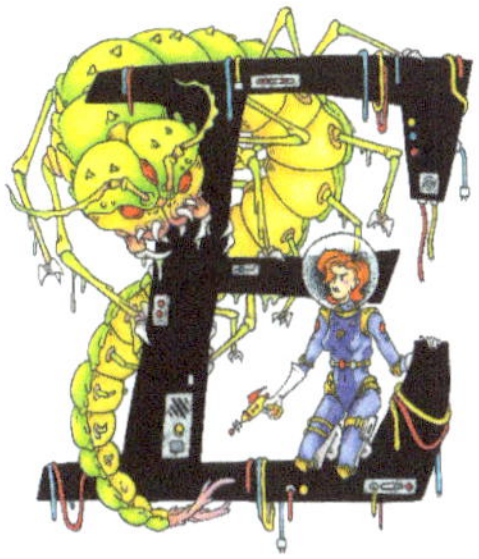
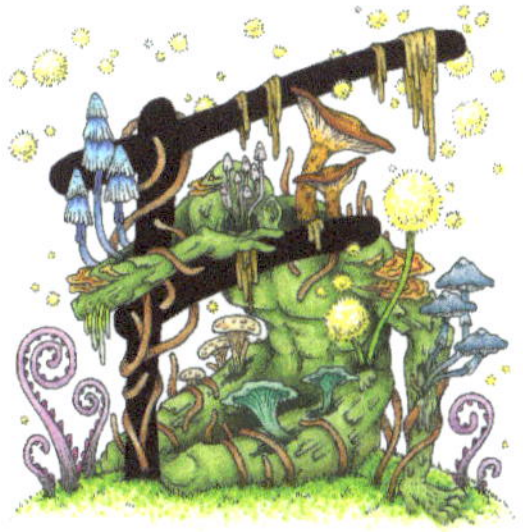
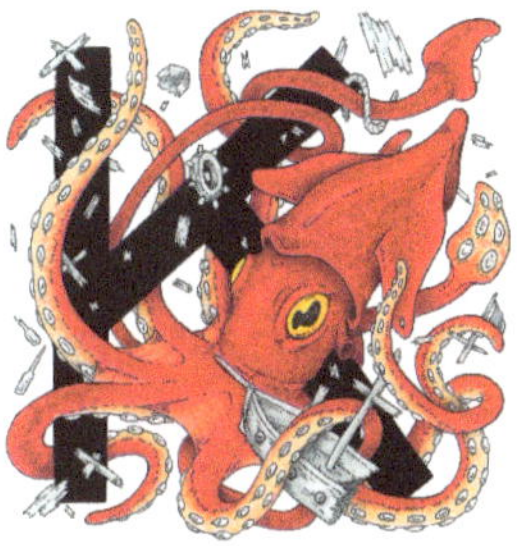
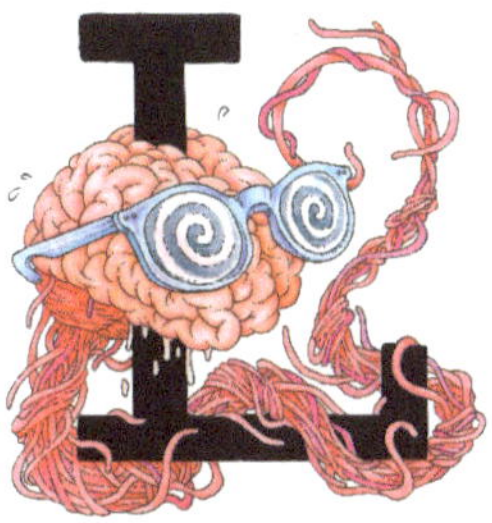
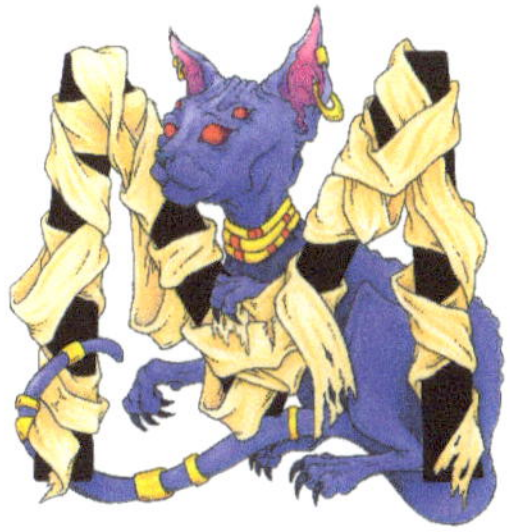
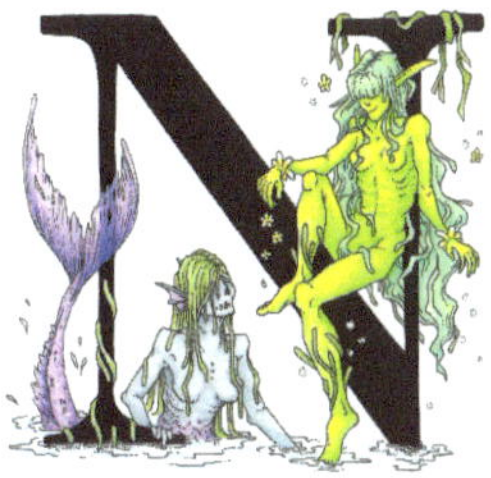
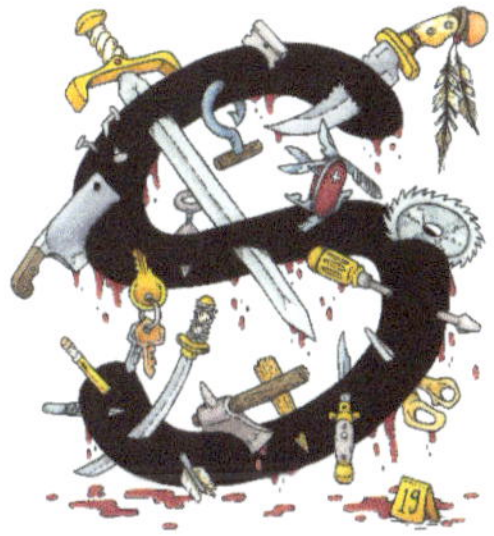
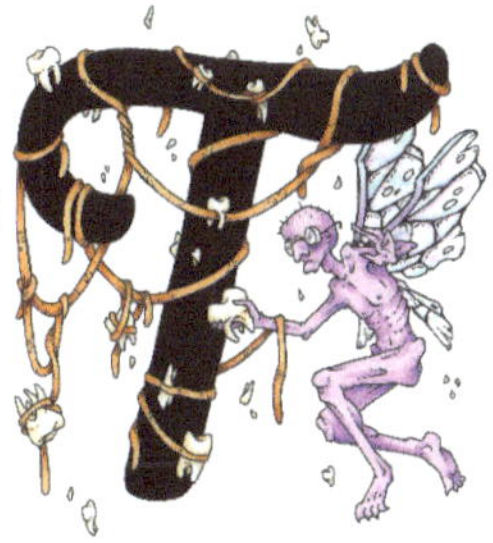
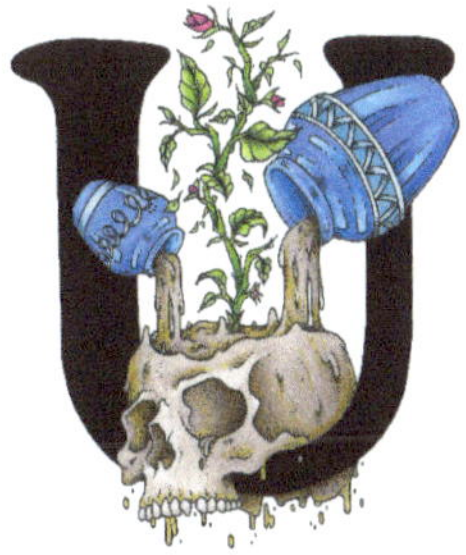
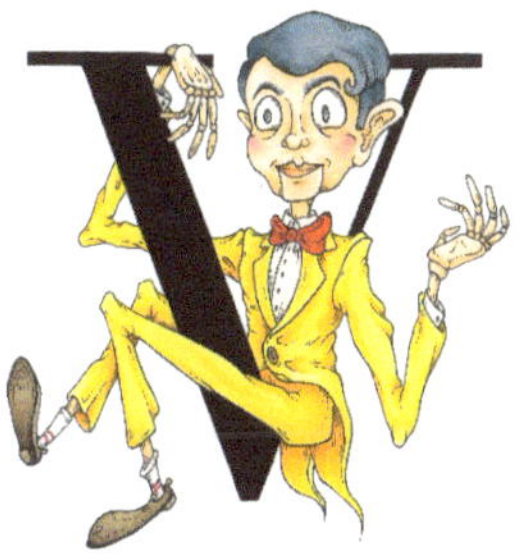
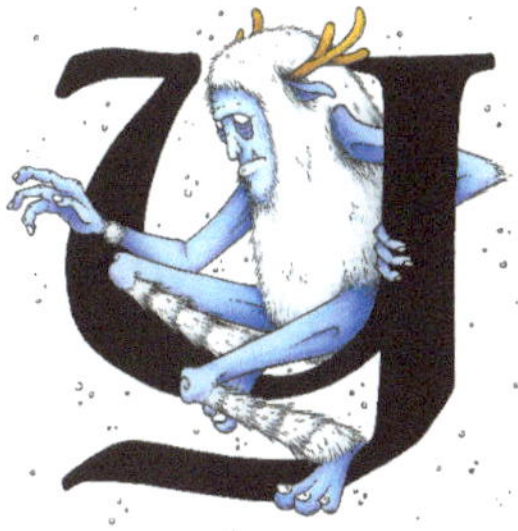
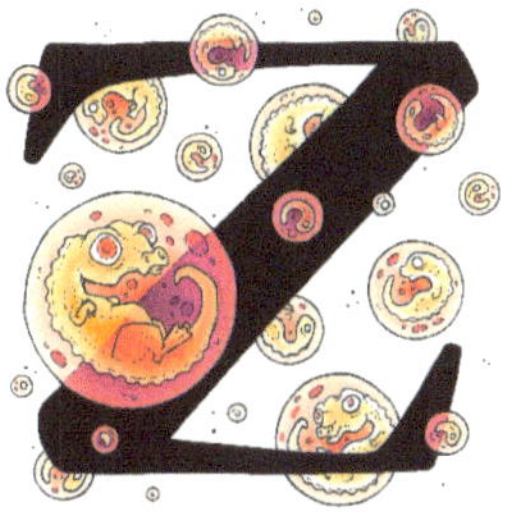

GOODBYE!

THE END

CPSIA information can be obtained
at www.ICGtesting.com
Printed in the USA
LVHW072031220121
677210LV00014B/189